1st AMERICAN: CHEROKEE

Ty 'GWY' Wilson

illustrated by JASMINE RIGGS

translated by ᏢᏓᏥ

This drawing by X

1st American: Cherokee

ISBN: 979-8-9889198-0-3
Printed in [USA]

"1st American" is a series of children's books that will help to preserve Native American languages. The introductory book of that series being "1st American Cherokee". This is a project of the CBIHP Foundation. *American rescue plan funding was provided in part by Oklahoma Humanities(OH) and the National Endowment for the Humanities(NEH).*

This book is dedicated to my recently deceased aunt Carmen Johnson,

Carmen was not a mother but she helped raise a lot of kids, including myself. She had a passion for inspiring & educating kids, and I hope this book does both of those.

Thank you Carm for always believing in me. I will miss and love you forever.

ᱠᱟᱰ

buffalo

ፈረስ

horse

GS

cow

chicken

eagle

elephant

or

butterfly

spider

Dəɹ

fish

bullfrog

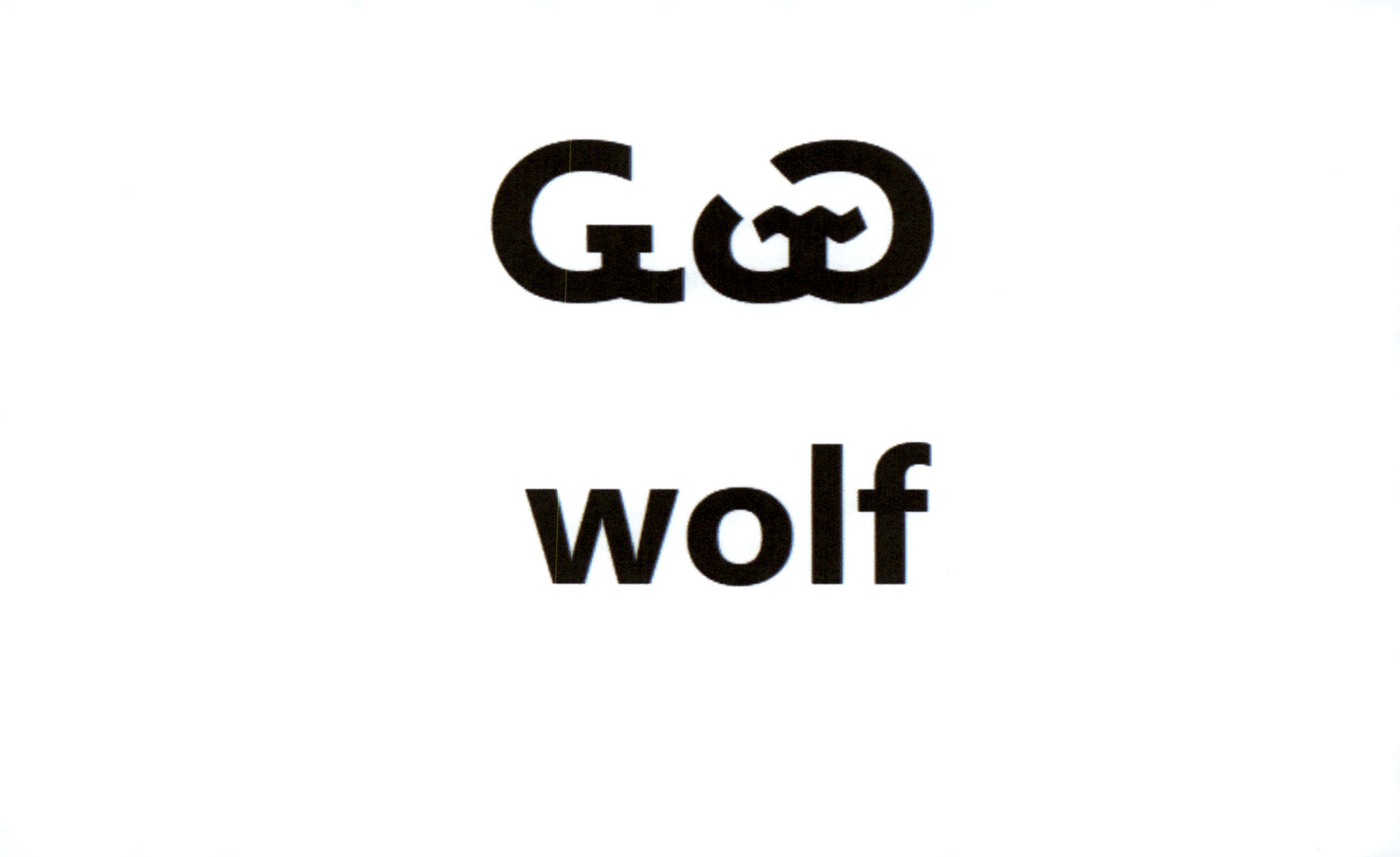

wolf

THE END

FLIP BOOK

THE

Ty 'GWY' Wilson

FLIP BOOK OVER

END

ᏩᏯ

wa-ya

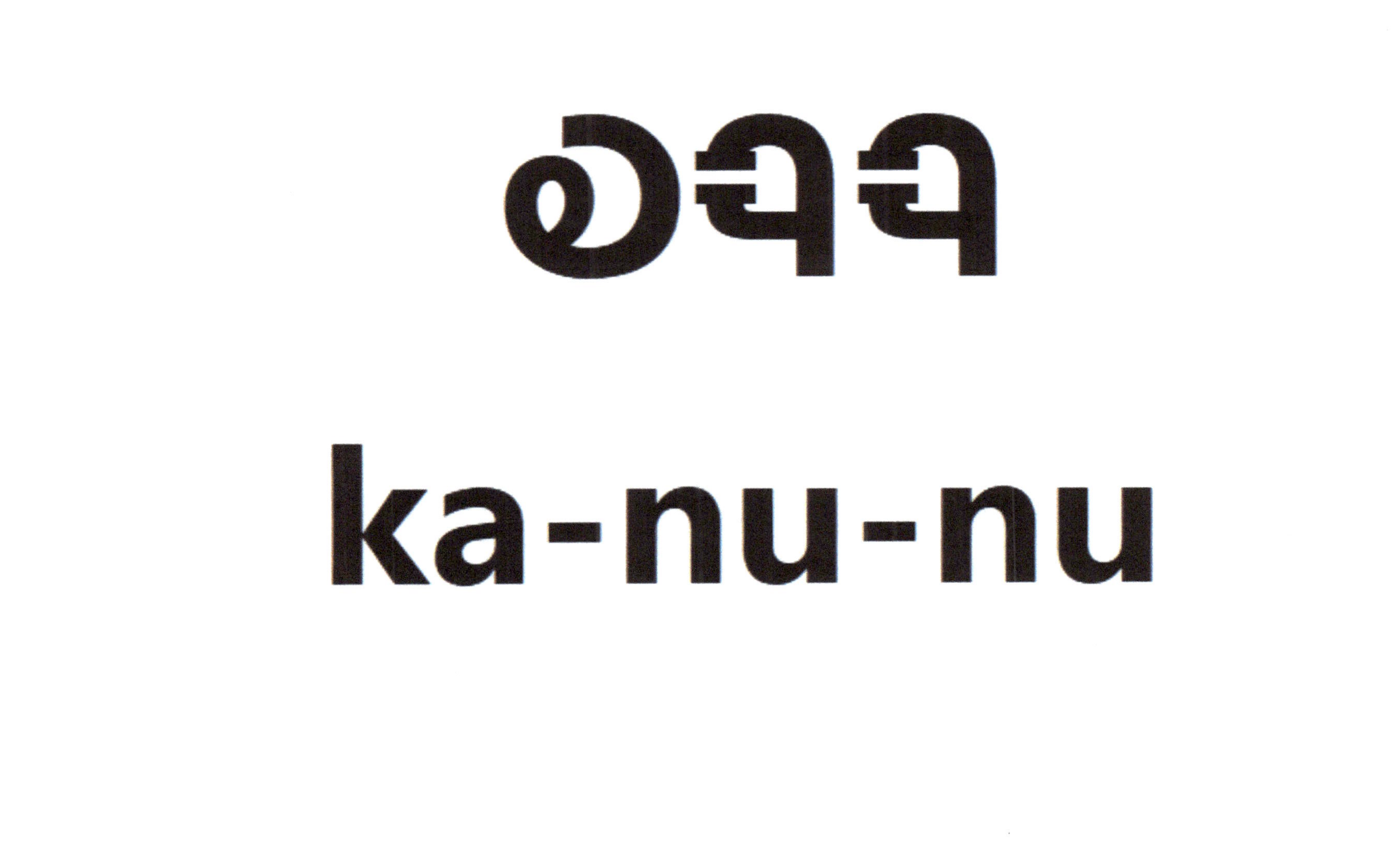

ka-nu-nu

ᎠᏣᏗ

a-tsa-di

ᎧᏁᏁᏍᎩ

ka-hna-ne-s-gi

ka-ma-ma

ᏬᎭᎵ

wo-ha-li

ᏥᏔᎦ

tsi-ta-ga

ᏩᎦ

wa-ga

ᏐᏈᎵ

so-qui-li

ᏯᎾᏌ

ya-na-sa

This book is dedicated to my recently deceased aunt Carmen Johnson,

Carmen was not a mother but she helped raise a lot of kids, including myself. She had a passion for inspiring & educating kids, and I hope this book does both of those.

Thank you Carm for always believing in me. I will miss and love you forever.

"1st American" is a series of children's books that will help to preserve Native American languages. The introductory book of that series being "1st American Cherokee". This is a project of the CBIHP Foundation. American rescue plan funding was provided in part by Oklahoma Humanities(OH) and the National Endowment for the Humanities(NEH).

1st American: Cherokee

ISBN: 979-8-9889198-0-3

Printed in [USA]

1st AMERICAN: CHEROKEE

Ty 'GWY' Wilson

illustrated by JASMINE RIGGS

translated by ᏢᏓᏥ

www.ingramcontent.com/pod-product-compliance
Lightning Source LLC
LaVergne TN
LVHW050948250826
846485LV00044B/1011
* 9 7 9 8 9 8 8 9 1 9 8 0 3 *